Stonehenge & Avebury

the greatest STONE CIRCLES in the WORLD

Facts you never knew about Avebury and Stonehenge, with a selection of
contemporary poetry and photographs by Michael Pitts

A vebury's *Great Stone Circle* is the best known structure in a landscape of monuments. Their true functions are not known, but are thought to have been religious and political.

The Circle was built 2500 BC, after the surrounding *ditch* and *bank*. Perhaps also made at this time were the *Cove* and *Obelisk Circles*, inside the Great Circle, and the *Beckhampton* and *West Kennet Avenues*, stone rows leading to it. At the end of the Kennet Avenue was the *Sanctuary*, rings of stone and wood together. *Silbury Hill* (2400 BC) is a large chalk mound. Two timber enclosures were built nearby at *West Kennet* (2000 BC).

Avebury League Team, 1905/6. Gillet Marlboro

Ancestors of the megalith builders dug large ditches on *Windmill Hill* (3500 BC), perhaps to defend a village. They were among the first farmers, rearing pigs, cattle and sheep and growing crops in gardens cleared from the old forest. The *West Kennet Long Barrow* was their greatest burial place.

The megaliths probably stood until the middle ages, when many were hidden below ground. Under the *Barber Stone* was found the skeleton of a travelling surgeon, killed when it was pushed over. Other stones were broken up in the eighteenth century with fire and water, and again in the last century with iron wedges. Houses and walls in the village are built from the pieces.

Stone Circles

Number About 700 have been found so far in the United Kingdom.

Largest diameter Avebury Great Circle: about 332m.

Second and third largest Cove and Obelisk Circles at Avebury: 103.6m.

Fourth largest Long Meg, Cumbria: about 101m.

Smallest Moor Divock, Cumbria: 2.7m.

Commonest number of stones in circle 12 (over 30 rings).

Largest number of stones Avebury Great Circle: estimated 98.

Tallest megalith Rudston, Humberside: over 7.9m (it's missing a bit from the top).

Number of stone circles with carvings 14.

Ruched in new green a line of hawthorns
fended the wind from us until, climbing
the earthwork's slope, we broke
into bareness, a wide stage, closeturfed,

spattered with April daisies, no bush or tree
standing against the wind, no boundary
but the edge, the drop to encircling farmland –
variegated, functional, the forest's

tamed successor. Now this height is the wilder;
unploughed ages lie deep over the scars
of hearths where the first ironmasters
made tools to ease their living and, in fear,

death's sharp instruments. In the Easter sunshine
we walked slowly, at ease, as if the Earth were safe.

Pamela Gillilan from
Iron Age (On Solsbury Hill).

Archaeologists at Avebury

Unlike at Stonehenge, where the ground has more holes than a bath sponge, archaeologists have been reluctant to dig up Avebury. Perhaps it's just too big.

John Aubrey Writer and antiquarian, discovered Avebury on horseback 1649. Guided Charles II up Silbury Hill.

William Stukeley Made detailed drawings and notes when many stones were being broken up, 1719–24. Left only record of Beckhampton Avenue, drawn "from top of an haycock". Thought Sanctuary (his name) temple to earth goddess and Avebury centre of Druidism and monument to our ancestors' piety. Also did good work at Stonehenge.

Harold St George Gray Directed first large excavations, 1908–22, digging into great ditch silts. Found bottom 9m below ground level, established rough date of site and uncovered only full human skeleton in circles (his "absence at breakfast was unfortunate, for the skull had been trampled upon before any part of it was actually recognised by the workmen"). Excellent survey.

Alexander Keiller As in marmalade. Bought Windmill Hill, excavations there 1925–29. Bought stone circles, more farmland and manor house. Restored half of Great Circle, removed trees and buildings and discovered buried megaliths, 1934–39. Locally famous for fast cars, strange happenings at manor and providing work when little was available. And why did he knock down all those houses?

Maud Cunnington Local archaeologist who found the Sanctuary with Stukeley's drawings, and dug most of it like potatoes, 1930. Finds records good, but survey hangs on precision of umbrella length.

Stuart Piggott Assistant to Keiller, later Professor of Archaeology at Edinburgh. Excavated West Kennet Long Barrow with Richard Atkinson 1955–56. Stukeley's biographer.

Cardiff University John Evans and Alasdair Whittle, assisted by colleagues and students, looking at ancient landscape and activities 1967 – present. Recent work includes major discoveries at West Kennet.

[3]
and can the stone know
me   I wonder
     does the stone
               wonder

even here   among absences
and wreckage

     if any place

[19]
bloody stone
     blood I am
grained
     with breath
death of ancestors
     of my blood
     stone I am

wizened

     enduring

          the sun's hammer
          the frost's nails
          the wind's arsenal

Richard Burns from **Avebury.**

Sunrise at the cove on midsummer day.

1. Three sere old 'moor' men – brooding; silent mock:
   they sit wreathed fast in swaythed 'clothed' crop
   of bell 'beauty's, mossing velvet' smock.
   Grown wind'worn, storm'torn, jag'gnawn –
   time's teeth paring stone. (Air'cup hone'
   heath'hollow, rack'rock winter moan).

2. A fragment 'fraught these sarsons': aught
   men's hope of number's scope, be saught
   where sun'fleet feeds earth's wombing' wrought …
   in pain, she lain …
             Her bain
   bore hoar'age granite's heaving rod
                       (his God)
   once raised, not now an even'memory's' sod

3. Though still stern'standing to an ancient grace:
   forever frowning; wisdom's face?
   If thought could only delve that secret: … find … the nature
   of their passing mind …

   But men are blind!

                    Graham Ovenden **The Old Stones.**

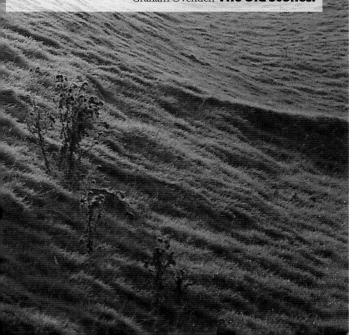

Life inside the rings
(at time of first printing)
Inhabitants 27 people, 9 dogs, 5
cats and 1 pony (the sheep are
only visiting).
Tallest person 1.84m (6' ½").
Tallest person in 1910 2.54m (8' 4").
Fred Kempster weighed 170kg
(27 stone or 380 lbs).
Telephones 29. *Bibles* 38.

Stones at Avebury
Tallest Two contenders, both of
which fell and broke in the 18th
century. 1. The Obelisk: about
6.5m long. 2. A stone at the north
entrance to the Great Circle: about
6.7m long.
Tallest standing At the north and south
entrances: about 4.25m above the
ground (one of these is known to
be 5.6m long).
Smallest Near the Obelisk: 2m above
ground level (full length 3m).
Carvings There aren't any. One stone
in the West Kennet Avenue has
hollows made by grinding stone
axeheads. Otherwise the stones are
completely unaltered natural slabs.

Buried People

The skeleton of a small adult (thought to be female) was found in the great ditch silts at Avebury in 1914. This burial has recently been dated to around 4100 years ago, some three centuries after the erection of the Great Stone Circle.

At about the same time as the Avebury woman died, the body of a 25–30 year old man was buried in the ditch at Stonehenge. The tips of two flint arrowheads were found in his bones: he had died violently.

These two are the only complete corpses found: but there is evidence for several other burials at both stone circles. At Avebury, where there has been very little excavation, fragments of human bone have been found near the foot of two megaliths, and in fourteen different places in the ditch silts.

At Stonehenge there has been more excavation, but most of it poorly recorded. Two apparent grave pits in the chalk have been found, one near the centre of the circles, the other outside the stones to the south east; the dates of these burials are not known. At least 25 of the Aubrey Holes (*see page* 14) had cremations put in them some time after they were first dug, and a further 30 cremations have been uncovered from the ditch and bank. Human bone fragments have also been found in the ditch.

More recent burials include the barber-surgeon at Avebury (apparently felled by a stone about AD 1320) and a skeleton in the top of the ditch at Stonehenge, thought by his excavator to be the hastily buried leftovers of an executed criminal. No-one seems to know how many modern Druid cremations have been secreted at Stonehenge.

We are the ones who once walked the paths you walked.
Set this down lest you forget.
We who once inhabited your planet.

In shoes of roots and leaf of web
We were one with nature's flow and ebb
and grass was then a gift of green abundance.

In shoes of twigs and shard of clay
We made our steps in the caterpillar's tracks
and followed the hedgehog's footprint of wonder.

See, we have left you
our shoes in enchanting circles.

John Agard **Earthwalk.**

They lie on short grass,
in a place where whiteness
builds hedges to filter the blue,
nowhere more than a dozen yards away.

Time eludes them.
Passing clouds have stained their backs
with unfelt shadow,
but otherwise nothing has moved.

Their small enclosure is the perfect frame
for all that a lengthy posture can express
of love or of strangeness,
two hands of cards disposed by careful hands
face down upon the turf,
as if in the expectation of return.

Peter Didsbury **The Sleepers.**

Stonehenge, with its horizontal ring supported by shaped megaliths, is unique. But what you see now is only the last stage in the story.

The first few stones, including the *Heel Stone*, were erected 3100 BC. Inside a *bank circle* were the *Aubrey Holes*, 56 pits now marked by white discs. Then light woodland grew when the site was abandoned for several centuries.

The new Stonehenge (2100 BC) was aligned on midsummer sunrise. A chalk *Avenue* ran from the old bank ring, and inside was erected a succession of stone monuments. Near the bank are the *Station Stones*. The massive *Sarsen Circle*, and smaller *Bluestone Circle* surround the *Sarsen Horseshoe* of five *Trilithons* (two

stones standing, one on top), the *Bluestone Horseshoe* and the single *Altar Stone*. Six centuries later, two rings of large pits (the Y and Z *holes*) were dug around the stones, and later still the Avenue was extended.

Around Stonehenge are sites with related religious and political meaning. The *Cursus*, a pair of long banks and ditches, was made at the time of the first Stonehenge. During the abandonment, a large "henge" was built at *Durrington Walls*, where a bank and internal ditch surrounded circular wooden constructions. Nearby was *Woodhenge*, six rings of posts with a grave in the middle, and at *Coneybury*, another small "henge". *Round barrows* surrounded the second Stonehenge, many of them covering graves containing valuable craft objects.

A game of Henge, my masters?
The pieces are set. We lost the box
with the instructions years ago.

Do you see Hangman? Or
Clock Patience? Building bricks
the gods grew out of? Dominoes?

Your move. You're in the ring —
of the hills, of the stones, of the walls
of your skull. You want to go?

You want out? Good. That's
the game. Whichever way you turn
are doors. Choose. Step through, so,

and whichever world you stumble
into will be different from all the others. Only
what *they* might have been,

                    you'll never know.

Philip Gross from **A Game of Henge.**

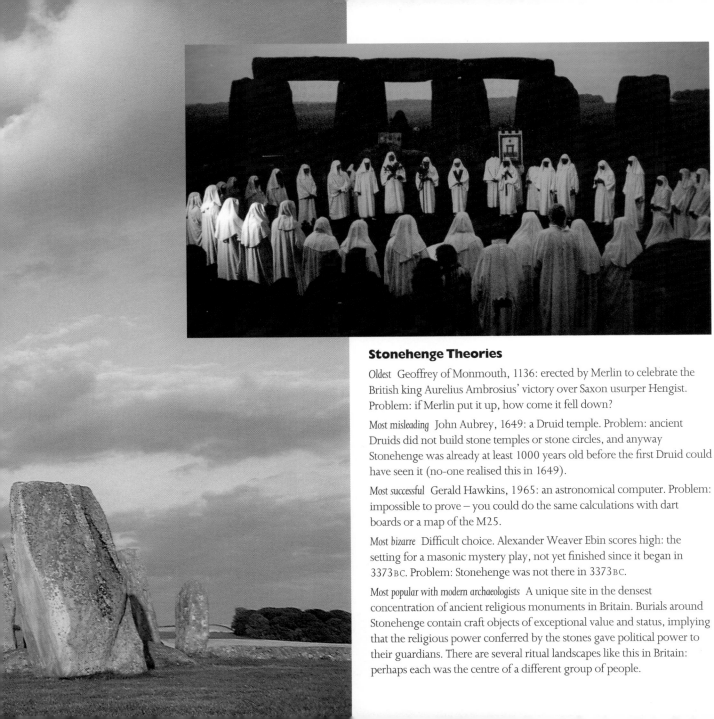

Stonehenge Theories

Oldest Geoffrey of Monmouth, 1136: erected by Merlin to celebrate the British king Aurelius Ambrosius' victory over Saxon usurper Hengist. Problem: if Merlin put it up, how come it fell down?

Most misleading John Aubrey, 1649: a Druid temple. Problem: ancient Druids did not build stone temples or stone circles, and anyway Stonehenge was already at least 1000 years old before the first Druid could have seen it (no-one realised this in 1649).

Most successful Gerald Hawkins, 1965: an astronomical computer. Problem: impossible to prove – you could do the same calculations with dart boards or a map of the M25.

Most bizarre Difficult choice. Alexander Weaver Ebin scores high: the setting for a masonic mystery play, not yet finished since it began in 3373 BC. Problem: Stonehenge was not there in 3373 BC.

Most popular with modern archaeologists A unique site in the densest concentration of ancient religious monuments in Britain. Burials around Stonehenge contain craft objects of exceptional value and status, implying that the religious power conferred by the stones gave political power to their guardians. There are several ritual landscapes like this in Britain: perhaps each was the centre of a different group of people.

Bare brown skeleton
my dear dead girl
those beads around your neck
cause me this pain
for your unspoken name.

I think if I look softly
I can see
within its bone-made cage
your young desire
a small and furry animal
stifled and stiff
among the scattered soil
and faint and quivering
the silver veins of spring's delight
you forfeited.

Before they laid you in your new
your glass and steel compartment
and lit you with a light that mocks the sun
my dead and nameless daughter,
may worm and root
and mould and mouse
have worked most perfectly
their secret alchemy
and freed your spirit for those corridors
where comets are its timekeepers.

And may the pinions of your soul
unseared by centuries' inevitable dust
beat unconfined by the curator's wire.

Eve Machin

Exhibit – Utrecht Museum.

Where do the Stones come from?

All the known megaliths at Avebury are sarsen, a very hard, locally present sandstone: there were around 600 altogether. The nearest source today for large sarsens is Piggledene, a valley 3½ km east of Avebury. However, 4500 years ago there may have been many large sarsens lying right where the stone rings and rows were built.

Most of the stones at Stonehenge are also sarsen (originally about 80 or more). These may have been brought from the Avebury area 27 km to the north. It is also possible that when Stonehenge was built, large sarsens lay on the ground in the vicinity.

More famous are the Stonehenge "bluestones", megaliths of non-local rock, of which 45 have so far been identified (including buried stumps). Except for the Altar Stone, a fallen sandstone slab nearly 5m long, the bluestones are all much smaller than the sarsens.

Moving the milestone.

Geologist William Judd suggested in 1902 that these alien stones reached Salisbury Plain in glaciers in the long distant past. Twenty years later, Herbert Thomas identified the source as south Wales, especially the Preseli Hills. He thought the stones were dragged and rafted from there to Wiltshire by the architects of Stonehenge, a theory widely accepted.

Now, however, ideas have changed again. The most detailed study ever done has recently been completed by a team at the Open University led by Richard Thorpe. They determined that most of the bluestones do indeed come from South Wales, but were almost certainly transported by glaciers some 400,000 years ago. The only stone at Stonehenge known to have been brought intentionally from Wales, is the one erected by English Heritage at the visitor reception area. This was donated by D G Williams, Lord of the Manor of Mynachlog-ddu, and was brought to the site in a lorry in 1989.

Two partly buried bluestones, one with a mortise hole just visible.

Uses for Megaliths at Stonehenge

Water purifier "It is generally averred hereabouts that pieces (or powder) of these stones putt into their Wells, doe drive away the Toades" (17th century).

Picnic shelter "A party of Goths lighted a fire against one of the stones and several fragments were broken off by the heat" (19th century).

Hoarding RADIO CAROLINE (painted in 1974) can still be read in lichen growth on the inside of one of the sarsens.

Vehicular support "One large stone was taken away to make a Bridge" (17th century).

Visitor book Before fenced in, the sarsens were grail to graffiti artists. Strange letters were found under a large fallen stone in 1861, and thought to be ancient: but it was later decided they were carved by a lithe itinerant mechanic.

Once upon a time a small
stone viaduct got bored
of going somewhere. It curled
up snug, forgetting all

about timetables and connections, so
its train of thought runs round
and round for ever and
its little whistle goes

who who

who who

who who

Philip Gross from
A Game of Henge.

Concrete stubs mark the post holes at Woodhenge.

Stones at Stonehenge

Tallest The two stones of the Great Trilithon: 6.7m above the ground (one is 9m long).

Smallest The western Station Stone: 1.2m high.

Carvings The best at any stone circle in Britain – although now very difficult to see (perhaps they were painted when new). At least four sarsens have engravings of groups of simple copper or bronze axeheads. There is an irregular rectangle shape on one of the big Trilithon stones; some archaeologists think this may be an image of a mother goddess (honest).